Fruit Without the Root

Why Not All Growth Is God-Grown

This book is for those who are no longer asking how far they can go,
but how faithfully they can stand.

It's not about "Is there fruit?"
It's about where—and how—it is rooted.

Cheri B

Fruit Without the Root: Why Not All Growth Is God-Grown

Published by Truths Coming Inc.

TruthsComing.com | CheriB.me

Print ISBN: 978-1-971522-08-1

Digital ISBN: 978-1-971522-06-7

First Edition: 2026

Scripture quotations are taken from the New American Standard Bible (NASB) unless otherwise noted. Hebrew and Greek word studies reference Strong's Exhaustive Concordance of the Bible.

Printed in the United States of America

*"Every plant which My heavenly Father did not plant
shall be uprooted."*

— Matthew 15:13

I would rather hear the drop of one tear
than see the shouts and praises of thousands.
Because one life truly changed
bears more fruit than a crowd impressed.

— Cheri B

Dedication

For those who chose roots when applause offered them branches.
For those who learned to wait when waiting was the harder thing.
For those who would rather be hidden by God
than displayed by man.

A Note Before You Begin

I did not set out to write a book about discernment.

I set out to ask the Lord why so many things that look fruitful do not last—and why some of the most rooted lives I know remain almost entirely unseen. The answer the Lord gave me, gently and over time, became these chapters.

I have tried to write this the way I have learned to walk with Him: slowly, with restraint, in a tone that does not strain to convince. If you sense an absence of urgency in these pages, that is intentional. Urgency is the language of fruit without root. Patience is the language of the soil where God Himself is working.

The Hebrew Scriptures and the Greek New Testament both carry depths that English translations cannot fully hold. I have tried, where I could, to draw from the original languages just enough to open a window into the Hebraic and apostolic mind—without weighing the text down. If those passages bless you, follow them deeper. The well does not run dry.

Most of all, this book was written from rest, and it asks to be read from rest. There is no rush. The truths gathered here have waited centuries. They will wait for the turning of one more page.

May the Lord plant whatever in this book is His, and uproot whatever is mine.

— Cheri B

Contents

Introduction

Growth is not the same as fruit.

And fruit is not proof of right planting.

In a world that measures success by speed, expansion, and what looks appealing, it is easy to mistake increase for approval. Ministries grow. Platforms expand. Influence multiplies. Yet Scripture warns us that not everything that grows has been planted by God.

Jesus did not ask whether something appeared fruitful. He spoke of roots. Of planting. Of what the Father Himself had established.

This book was not written to critique others, expose movements, or measure ministries. It was written to invite discernment—first in the heart, then in the soil where we allow our lives to take root.

Some growth is accelerated by pressure rather than obedience. Some fruit is sustained by systems rather than surrender. And some structures stand tall for a season, only to reveal shallow foundations when testing comes.

The question before us is not, *Is there fruit?*

The question is, *Who planted it—and what is feeding it?*

There is a Hebrew way of seeing that the West has largely forgotten. The ancient mind did not separate the seen from the unseen, the visible from the hidden, the harvest from the soil. To the Hebrew, a tree was never just its branches. A tree was its root system, its season, its source of water, the soil it had been placed in, and the years it had quietly endured before anyone tasted its fruit.

We have lost much of that vision.

We measure trees by their crowns. God measures them by their depth.

This book is for those who have learned that faithfulness often looks quieter than success, slower than ambition, and deeper than appearance. For those who would rather be rooted in truth than elevated by approval.

What the Father plants, remains.

What He does not plant, will not.

This is not a call to retreat from growth—but to return to the root.

Tone

Calm, not confrontational

Clear, not provocative

Discerning, not defensive

Grounded, not speculative

This book speaks from rest, not reaction.

What This Book Offers

This book offers to:

- Help you discern the difference between visible growth and formed growth
- Give language to instincts you already feel but haven't named
- Strengthen those who have chosen depth over exposure
- Clarify why some success feels hollow—even when it looks good
- Protect you from confusing momentum with obedience

This book does not offer to:

- Entertain
- Convince the unwilling
- Debate public opinion
- Offer shortcuts
- Affirm growth that bypasses formation

This book is written for readers who value integrity over immediacy and roots over recognition.

C h a p t e r   O n e

When Fruit Appears Too Soon

Growth is not proof of health.

In a world that celebrates visibility, we have learned to mistake appearance for maturity. We reward what looks appealing, what multiplies quickly, what draws attention, what produces visible results—often without asking what is sustaining it beneath the surface.

Fruit is compelling.

Roots are quiet.

Scripture never teaches us to chase fruit. It teaches us to abide.

John 15:4–6

"Abide in Me, and I in you. As the branch cannot bear fruit of itself unless it abides in the vine, so neither can you unless you abide in Me. I am the vine, you are the branches; he who abides in Me and I in him, he bears much fruit, for apart from Me you can do nothing. If anyone does not abide in Me, he is thrown away as a branch and dries up; and they gather them, and cast them into the fire and they are burned."

The word *abide* in this passage is the Greek *menō* (Strong's G3306). It means *to remain, to dwell, to continue, to be held.* It is not the language of activity. It is the language of staying. Of refusing to be moved. *Menō* is what a tenant does in a house—he occupies it. It is what a covenant partner does in a relationship—he keeps faith with it through every season.

Jesus did not say, *produce* fruit. He said, *abide*—and the fruit will follow.

This is the inversion the modern church has missed.

Yet many have learned to cultivate outcomes without submitting to formation, to display gifts without embracing obedience, and to gather influence without carrying responsibility. What grows fast may look impressive, but not everything that grows is meant to remain.

Fruit without a root does not always fail immediately.

It fails eventually.

That delay is what makes discernment difficult.

Some fruit looks convincing.

Some success feels anointed.

Some growth attracts affirmation, opportunity, and applause.

But time always reveals origin.

The Hebrew word for fruit is *peri* (פְּרִי, Strong's H6529). It comes from a root meaning *to bear, to bring forth, to be fruitful*. But what is striking in the Hebrew Scriptures is how often *peri* is paired with *shoresh* (שֹׁרֶשׁ, Strong's H8328)—the word for *root*. In Hebraic thought, fruit is never separated from its source. A tree without roots is not a tree at all. It is a cut branch lying on the ground, sustained by the moisture it carried with it—alive for a moment, then dry.

Isaiah understood this. So did Jeremiah. So did Hosea. The prophets did not look at a nation's harvest to determine its health—they looked at its hidden places.

This book is not written to expose people—it is written to expose processes. It is not meant to shame growth, but to question what kind. It is not an argument against fruit, but a return to order.

Roots grow underground by design. They form in darkness, pressure, and waiting. They take time. They require submission to seasons that cannot be rushed or displayed.

Fruit that appears before this work is complete may still look good—but it cannot carry weight, withstand heat, or remain when conditions change.

The question is not, *Is there fruit?*

The question is, *What is it rooted in?*

This book is for those who are no longer impressed by speed, trendiness, visibility, or scale—and also for those who are willing to slow down long enough to tell the difference between what is growing and what is simply showing.

There is one moment in the Gospels that captures this tension as clearly as any.

Jesus was on His way into Jerusalem, hungry. He saw a fig tree in full leaf and approached it expecting fruit. But when He arrived, the tree had nothing but leaves—because, Mark tells us, *it was not the season for figs* (Mark 11:13).

And then Jesus did something that has puzzled readers for two thousand years.

He cursed it.

May no one ever eat fruit from you again.

Why?

Because in the Hebraic agricultural mind, a fig tree in full leaf was *making a claim*. The early figs—called *paggim*—appeared *before* the leaves on a healthy tree. A tree displaying full foliage without fruit was advertising a harvest it did not actually have. It looked alive. It looked productive. But the appearance was a lie.

Jesus did not curse a tree for being barren in the wrong season.

He cursed a tree for *displaying what it could not produce.*

This is the parable of fruit without the root in living form.

And it is no accident that immediately after this, Jesus walked into the Temple and overturned the tables. The two acts were one act. The fig tree and the Temple were both showing leaves. Both had become impressive at a distance. Both had ceased to bear what they advertised.

Display is not fruit.

Foliage is not formation.

And the Lord, who is patient with barrenness, is not patient with pretense.

Chapter Two

Roots Are Formed in Secret

Most roots are not impressive.

They do not announce themselves. They do not draw attention. Majority of roots do not multiply visibly or quickly. Most of their work happens unseen, below the surface, in conditions that would feel unproductive—or even discouraging—if measured by appearance alone.

This is by design.

In Scripture, God consistently chooses hidden places for formation. Wilderness before promise. Obscurity before authority. Waiting before fruit. What grows too quickly above ground often lacks the depth to endure what comes next.

Jeremiah 17:7–8

"Blessed is the man who trusts in the Lord and whose trust is the Lord. For he will be like a tree planted by the water, that extends its roots by a stream and will not fear when the heat comes; but its leaves will be green, and it will not be anxious in a year of drought nor cease to yield fruit."

The Hebrew word for *planted* in this passage is *shathal* (שָׁתַל, Strong's H8362). It is not a passive word. *Shathal* means *to be transplanted by intention, to be set in place with purpose*. It is the word a gardener uses when he chooses where a tree will grow—not where it sprouted by accident, but where it has been deliberately placed.

There is a different Hebrew word for a tree that simply springs up—*tsamach* (צָמַח, Strong's H6779). That word describes natural emergence. But *shathal* is covenantal. It is the word for a tree the Master Himself has set in soil He has chosen.

You are not where you are by accident.

Roots require pressure.

They require time and nourishment.

They require submission to seasons that cannot be rushed or replicated.

This is why true formation often feels slow.

Look at Paul. Converted between 33 and 36 AD on the road to Damascus, he then disappeared. Galatians tells us he went into Arabia, returned to Damascus, and only after three years went up to Jerusalem to see Peter for fifteen days. From there he went into the regions of Syria and Cilicia, largely unknown to the churches of Judea. It was somewhere between ten and fourteen years from his encounter on that road before he stepped into the apostolic ministry the church now associates with his name. The man who would write nearly half the New Testament spent more than a decade in obscurity first.

Look at David. He was around fifteen years old when Samuel poured the oil over his head in his father's house. Then he fled from Saul. He hid in caves. He lived among enemies. He led a band of distressed and indebted men in the wilderness for ten to fifteen years before he sat on the throne of Judah, and another seven and a half years before he was crowned over all Israel. He was already in his thirties when the kingdom God had promised him in his teens finally came into his hands.

Two of the most consequential lives in Scripture were marked young and elevated late.

We live in a culture that rewards immediacy. Speed is celebrated as wisdom. Visibility is confused with favor. But growth that bypasses formation is fragile, even when it looks strong.

Calling may come quickly, but preparation comes slowly—and promotion comes at the appointed time.

Roots do not hurry to be seen.

They hurry to be secure.

Many misunderstand this phase because it offers little external feedback. There is no applause underground. No metrics. No affirmation. Only quiet obedience and consistency when nothing seems to be happening.

There is always a gap between oil and throne—between encounter and assignment. The anointing marks you. The wilderness forms you into someone who can carry it.

Yet this is where stability is built.

The ancient near-eastern farmer understood something modern eyes have lost. In the dry hill country of Judea, a tree's survival depended almost entirely on what no one could see. A fig tree could stand four feet tall above the soil and have a root system reaching twenty feet down to find water. The visible portion was almost incidental. What mattered—what determined whether the tree would still be alive after a season of drought—was the patient, unseen labor of the roots reaching into the dark for living water.

A tree that survives storms does not do so because of its height, but because of its depth. When pressure comes—when heat intensifies, when winds increase—it is the unseen structure that determines what remains.

Oak trees, for all their strength, are known to topple in windy conditions because they tend toward shallow roots. The trunk is impressive. The canopy is wide. But the root system never went deep enough to anchor what stood above it. This is a season to be thankful to God for cultivating us with deeper roots—for the slow, often uncomfortable work He is doing below the surface that no storm will be able to reach.

This is why God often delays exposure.

Not as punishment.

Not as withholding.

But as protection.

Premature visibility can crush what has not yet been strengthened. Responsibility introduced before capacity creates strain. Influence granted before character produces fracture. What looks like favor on the surface can become a burden underneath if the root system is shallow.

This is also why comparison is dangerous in seasons of formation.

You cannot measure your progress by someone else's visibility. You cannot judge your obedience by another person's acceleration. Roots do not grow on the same timeline, and they do not respond to pressure in identical ways.

What matters is not how quickly something appears, but how deeply it is anchored.

Some of the most important work you will ever do will feel unnoticed, uncelebrated, and even unnecessary to others. That does not mean it is insignificant. It means it is foundational.

Roots are formed in secret so fruit can remain in public.

If this season feels quiet, resist the urge to force growth you are not yet meant to sustain. What is rooted well will not need to prove itself later.

Consider the mustard seed.

Jesus chose this image deliberately. *The kingdom of heaven is like a mustard seed, which a man took and sowed in his field; and this is smaller than all other seeds, but when it is full grown, it is larger than the garden plants and becomes a tree* (Matthew 13:31–32).

What He did not say in that parable, but every farmer in His audience already knew, was this: a mustard seed sits in the dark for weeks before anything visible happens. There is no faster path. The seed cannot be hurried. The work below ground precedes the work above it, and no amount of staring at the soil makes the sprout come faster.

In the kingdom, hiddenness is not a delay. It is the *first half* of the work.

Chapter Three

Formation Is Not Performance

Performance is visible.

Formation is not.

Performance is rewarded quickly.

Formation is rarely noticed while it is happening.

This is where many become confused.

We have learned to measure readiness by output rather than by depth. We assume that because something can be done publicly, it must have been formed privately. But Scripture never equates ability with maturity, nor visibility with preparation.

A person can function long before they are formed.

Gifts often emerge before character is settled. Influence can arrive before wisdom. Opportunity can precede discernment. When this happens, performance fills the gap that formation was meant to occupy.

At first, performance can look convincing.

It speaks the right language.

It produces measurable results.

It gathers affirmation and momentum.

But performance is sustained by energy, not by endurance.

Formation, on the other hand, reshapes the inner life. It works on motives rather than outcomes. It confronts impatience, pride, and the desire to be seen. It teaches restraint, submission, and faithfulness when no one is watching.

Colossians 2:6–7

"Therefore as you have received Christ Jesus the Lord, so walk in Him, having been firmly rooted and now being built up in Him and established in your faith, just as you were instructed, and overflowing with gratitude."

The Greek word translated *firmly rooted* is *rhizoō* (Strong's G4492). It is a perfect passive participle—meaning the rooting has already taken place and continues to hold. Paul is not describing an activity the believer performs. He is describing a condition the believer has been brought into. The roots are not something we manufacture. They are something we submit to.

Formation is what God does to us in the soil where He has placed us.

Performance is what we do when we are uncertain whether the soil is enough.

This is why formation often feels uncomfortable.

Performance allows control.

Formation requires surrender.

Performance asks, *How did this look?*

Formation asks, *What did this cost?*

Performance can be replicated.

Formation cannot.

One of the clearest signs that formation is incomplete is the need to continually prove oneself. When identity is not yet rooted, affirmation becomes fuel. Without it, confidence falters. Without recognition, motivation weakens.

Formation removes that dependence.

When a person has been formed, they no longer need constant confirmation that what they are doing matters. They just know. They have settled it privately. Their obedience is not contingent on response.

This does not mean they withdraw from public life. It means they are no longer driven by it.

Performance seeks exposure.

Formation can withstand obscurity.

This distinction becomes especially important when growth accelerates.

Rapid expansion amplifies what already exists beneath the surface. If insecurity remains, it will surface under pressure. If pride is unaddressed, it will harden when challenged. If obedience is conditional, it will fracture when the cost increases.

Formation prepares a person to carry success without being reshaped by it.

This is why God often allows performance to plateau.

Not to frustrate progress, but to protect the person. A pause can reveal whether someone is rooted or merely driven. When momentum slows, formation continues to work—if it is allowed.

Those who mistake formation for delay will attempt to replace it with activity. They will create movement to avoid stillness. They will produce output to silence the discomfort of waiting.

But activity is not formation.

Busyness is not obedience.

There is a Hebrew principle woven through the Torah called *tikun*—a slow, patient repair. The rabbis taught that God does not heal the way the world heals. The world heals quickly, scarred. God heals slowly, whole. Formation is *tikun*—the unhurried mending of the inner man before the outer man is asked to carry weight.

What is formed slowly will last longer than what is built quickly. Performance may open doors, but formation determines what happens once you walk through them.

If you find yourself tempted to prove rather than to abide, return to the work beneath the surface. There is no shortcut that produces lasting strength.

Formation always outlives performance.

The only true performance is the one where God promotes because of faithful formation.

There is a small word in the Hebrew Scriptures that captures formation in a single syllable: *tov* (טוֹב, Strong's H2896).

Tov is what God said over each day of creation. *And God saw that it was tov.* It is most often translated *good*, but the Hebrew word means more than moral approval. *Tov* means *fitted for its purpose, functional, in right relationship to what it was made for.*

A thing is *tov* when it is doing what it was made to do.

Formation is the slow process of becoming *tov*—of being shaped into the kind of vessel that fits the purpose for which God made it. Performance can imitate function. Only formation produces *tov*.

And on the day God finishes His formation work in you, He will say of you what He said over the original creation: *Tov me'od.* Very good.

C h a p t e r   F o u r

The Branch

There are moments in Scripture where a single word carries the weight of a chapter.

Zechariah 6:12 is one of those moments.

Zechariah 6:12

"Then say to him, 'Thus says the Lord of hosts, "Behold, a man whose name is Branch, for He will branch out from where He is; and He will build the temple of the Lord."'"

The word *Branch* is spoken twice in this verse. The first as identity. The second as function.

The Hebrew word used is *tsemach* (צֶמַח, Strong's H6780).

It means: *a sprout, a shoot, that which springs forth, growth rising from the ground.*

This word does not describe something manufactured, forced, or displayed for approval.

It describes life that emerges because it is alive.

A *tsemach* does not strain to grow.

It does not announce itself.

It does not compete.

It rises quietly—from what was hidden—because God causes it to rise.

Scripture uses *tsemach* prophetically to describe the Messiah:

One who would not come in spectacle, but in righteous growth.

One whose authority would emerge from obedience, not ambition.

Isaiah called Him a *tender shoot* (Isaiah 53:2)—a *yoneq* growing out of dry ground. Jeremiah called Him a *righteous Branch* (Jeremiah 23:5)—a *tsemach tsaddiq*. Zechariah, here, says simply, *Behold the man whose name is Branch.*

He did not arrive on a wave. He emerged from the soil.

This is why the word *Branch* is repeated in Zechariah.

The first time speaks to identity:

"His name is the Branch."

The second speaks to function:

"From His place He shall branch out."

Who He is and what He does are the same.

This is one of the most quietly radical truths in all of Scripture.

In our culture, identity and function are often divorced. A person becomes one thing on a platform and another thing at home. A leader projects one image to followers and lives by another rule in private. The branch we are shown in public is grafted onto a different root than the one we walk in alone.

This is not how the Messiah came.

He was the Branch in the wilderness. He was the Branch in the synagogue. He was the Branch on the cross. He was the Branch alone in the garden, sweat falling like blood. There was no separation between what He carried and who He was.

This reveals a vital truth:

Fruit is never the root.

Growth flows from identity, not effort.

True fruit is not produced by striving to appear fruitful.

It is the natural result of being rooted where God has planted you.

The Branch does not grow outward first—

He grows upward from what was hidden.

And so do we.

There is more woven into the word *tsemach* than a single chapter can hold.

In the prophets, *tsemach* becomes a Messianic title. Jeremiah calls Him *Tsemach Tsaddiq*—the Righteous Branch (Jeremiah 23:5). Zechariah calls Him simply *Tsemach*, the Branch (Zechariah 3:8; 6:12). Isaiah, using a slightly different image but the same idea, calls Him *netzer*—a tender shoot (Isaiah 11:1) and *yoneq*, a young plant (Isaiah 53:2).

Four prophets, four images, one truth: the Messiah comes up from the ground.

Not down from the sky in triumph. Not in from the desert in fury. Up from the ground, like a green thing pressing through soil that no one was watching.

This is the deepest pattern in Scripture, and we miss it constantly.

We expect God to descend.

He keeps choosing to *emerge*.

From a barren womb. From a manger. From an obscure village. From a working-class trade. From a courtroom that condemned Him. From a tomb sealed with a stone. From every place that looked finished, the *tsemach* kept rising.

And He is doing the same in His people.

The work that is being done in your hidden season is *tsemach* work. It is the slow, unforced, upward pressing of life that has been planted by God Himself. You do not need to manufacture it. You do not need to announce it. You do not need to compare its rate of emergence to anyone else's.

Tsemach does not race.

Tsemach rises.

C h a p t e r   F i v e

When God Delays Exposure

Delay is often misunderstood.

We assume that if something is meant to grow, it should appear quickly. If it does not, we begin to question timing, direction, or calling. But Scripture repeatedly shows that delay is not absence—it is intention.

God delays exposure not because He is uncertain, but because He is precise.

Exposure magnifies whatever already exists. It amplifies strength, but it also magnifies weakness. What has not yet been strengthened in private will be strained in public. What has not yet been settled internally will be tested externally.

This is why delay is often an act of mercy.

Before Joseph was elevated, he was hidden. Before David was crowned, he was overlooked. Before Jesus began public ministry, He lived in obscurity. These were not wasted years. They were formative years.

Joseph was thirty when he stood before Pharaoh. David was thirty when he was finally crowned over all Israel. Jesus was thirty when the heavens opened over the Jordan. The Hebrew tradition recognized thirty as the age of full priestly maturity—the age at which a Levite could enter into the full weight of his service.

What was God doing in those hidden years?

He was building men whose roots could carry their crowns.

Delay protects identity.

When exposure comes too early, identity becomes entangled with response. Approval begins to shape decisions. Criticism begins to destabilize confidence. The inner life becomes reactive rather than rooted.

Delay allows identity to be anchored somewhere deeper.

In hidden seasons, obedience is purified. Motives are examined. Faithfulness is tested without reward. This is where calling is clarified—not by affirmation, but by endurance.

Delay also protects others.

Unformed leadership harms more than the person carrying it. Influence given before discernment can misdirect people. Authority assumed without humility can wound communities. Delay gives time for wisdom to mature so that responsibility is carried with care.

This is why impatience is dangerous.

Impatience interprets delay as denial. It looks for alternatives. It manufactures opportunities. It forces doors that were meant to open naturally. In doing so, it often bypasses the very preparation that would have made the next season sustainable.

There is a Hebrew word for waiting that is unlike our English word. It is *qavah* (קָוָה, Strong's H6960). It does not simply mean *to pass time*. It means *to bind together by twisting, to gather strength like a cord woven of many strands*. The waiter is not idle. He is being woven.

Isaiah uses this word: *Those who wait* (qavah) *upon the Lord shall renew their strength*. The renewal is not separate from the waiting—it is *because* of it. The cord becomes stronger as more strands are added.

The waiter becomes stronger as more days are added. Delay is not the suspension of the work. Delay *is* the work.

God's timing is rarely fast, but it is always accurate.

Exposure is not the goal—faithfulness is.

When exposure finally comes, those who have been formed by delay are not disoriented by it. They are not intoxicated by visibility or threatened by scrutiny. They have already settled who they are when no one was watching.

Delay teaches a person how to remain steady when attention arrives.

If you are in a season where growth feels hidden, resist the urge to interpret that as stagnation. What feels like stillness may be strengthening what will soon be required to hold weight.

What God delays, He is often deepening.

And what is deepened in secret will not collapse when it is seen.

Habakkuk 2:2–3

"Then the Lord answered me and said, 'Record the vision and inscribe it on tablets, that the one who reads it may run. For the vision is yet for the appointed time; it hastens toward the goal and it will not fail. Though it tarries, wait for it; for it will certainly come, it will not delay.'"

The appointed time. In Hebrew, *mo'ed* (מוֹעֵד, Strong's H4150). It is the same word used for the appointed feasts of the Lord—the Sabbath, Passover, Shavuot, the Day of Atonement. *Mo'ed* is not arbitrary time. It is *kairos* time. Set time. Time the Father Himself has marked on the calendar of heaven.

What God has marked, He will not miss.

And what He delays, He delays toward a *mo'ed* you cannot yet see.

Joseph stood in front of his brothers, years after they had thrown him in a pit and sold him into slavery, and said one of the most stunning sentences in all of Scripture: *You meant evil against me, but God meant it for good* (Genesis 50:20).

The Hebrew word for *meant* is the same in both halves of the sentence: *chashav* (חָשַׁב, Strong's H2803)—*to weave, to plan, to think with intent.* The brothers wove a plan. God wove a different one *through* their plan, using the same threads, producing a different garment.

Every hidden year Joseph spent—every false accusation, every forgotten promise, every iron prison wall—was a thread in a weaving he could not see while it was happening.

Delay, in the hand of God, is never wasted material. It is the loom on which the next season is being made.

Chapter Six

The Seduction of Visible Success

Visible success is persuasive.

It carries the appearance of validation. It signals progress. It suggests that something is working—and that assumption alone is often enough to silence discernment.

Success does not need to announce itself loudly to be seductive. Its power lies in how easily it can be trusted without being examined.

When something grows quickly, draws attention, or produces results, we instinctively assume health. We associate increase with approval and expansion with right direction. But Scripture never teaches that success is proof of alignment.

Success can coexist with immaturity.

Momentum can mask fragility.

Affirmation can replace discernment.

This is where many lose their footing.

Visible success creates pressure to maintain appearances. Once something is seen as effective, the fear of losing it begins to shape decisions. Adjustments are made to preserve growth rather than to protect integrity. Subtle compromises are justified in the name of impact.

What began in obedience can slowly shift into management.

The seduction is not always intentional. Often it is gradual. A person begins responding to expectation instead of instruction. They prioritize what works over what is true. They confuse influence with assignment.

Success then becomes the standard rather than faithfulness.

One of the dangers of visible success is that it accelerates imitation. Others want to replicate the outcome without understanding the process. Methods are copied. Language is borrowed. Appearances are reproduced—while formation is ignored.

This creates fruit without roots.

The result may look similar on the surface, but it lacks the resilience to endure pressure. When conditions change—when attention shifts, when resistance increases, when cost rises—what was built on appearance begins to falter.

Matthew 7:16–20

"You will know them by their fruits. Grapes are not gathered from thorn bushes nor figs from thistles, are they? So every good tree bears good fruit, but the bad tree bears bad fruit. A good tree cannot produce bad fruit, nor can a bad tree produce good fruit. Every tree that does not bear good fruit is cut down and thrown into the fire. So then, you will know them by their fruits."

The Greek word for *know* in this passage is *epiginōskō* (Strong's G1921)—a word that means *to know fully, to recognize, to come to understand by careful examination*. It is not the casual *ginōskō* of passing acquaintance. It is the searching knowledge of one who has looked closely at the source.

Jesus did not say, *You will be impressed by their fruit*. He said, *You will know them by examining it carefully*.

The fruit was never meant to be admired from a distance. It was meant to be tested.

Another danger of success is that it can drown out warning signs.

When something is growing, it is harder to question it. When people are responding, it feels unwise to slow down. When affirmation is constant, correction can feel unnecessary or even threatening.

But success does not eliminate the need for discernment. It increases it.

Not every door that opens is meant to be walked through.

Not every opportunity is aligned with assignment.

Not every increase is sustainable.

The question is not, *Is this successful?*

The question is, *Is this being sustained by obedience?*

True success does not require constant reinforcement. It does not demand protection from scrutiny. It does not collapse when applause fades.

What is rooted deeply can bear visibility without being reshaped by it.

Visible success becomes dangerous only when it is trusted more than truth.

If success begins to require compromise, it is no longer serving its purpose. If growth demands constant performance, it is no longer healthy. If momentum replaces listening, it is no longer aligned.

Fruit that is God-grown does not need to be defended.

It remains—even when conditions are no longer favorable.

There is a Hebrew warning that runs through the wisdom literature: *Pride goes before destruction, and a haughty spirit before stumbling* (Proverbs 16:18).

The Hebrew word for *pride* there is *gaon* (גָּאוֹן, Strong's H1347), which can also be translated *swelling* or *exaltation*. The image is of something puffing up beyond its actual size. Of course, that which has been inflated must eventually deflate. Air does not stay in a balloon forever.

Visible success, when not anchored in formation, behaves the same way. It puffs up. It swells. It looks larger than it is. And the higher it rises on borrowed air, the harder the fall when reality returns.

Chapter Seven

Anointing Is Not Assignment

Many desire to become the next recognizable name—whether the next megachurch, evangelist, prophet, or even worship leader. Visibility is often mistaken for calling, and influence for assignment.

In this pursuit, anointing is treated as permission rather than power to steward. The ability to be seen is confused with the responsibility to be faithful.

But God's order is often inverted. Those who hurry toward prominence may find themselves misplaced, while those content to remain unseen are often entrusted with what lasts.

Matthew 19:30

"But many who are first will be last; and the last, first."

Anointing enables.

Assignment directs.

Confusing the two creates exhaustion.

The Hebrew word for *anoint* is *mashach* (מָשַׁח, Strong's H4886)—the same root from which we get *Mashiach*, Messiah, the Anointed One. Literally, it means *to smear, to consecrate, to set apart by the pouring of oil.* The act of anointing in Scripture was always tied to a specific function. Priests were anointed *for the altar.* Kings were anointed *over a particular tribe or kingdom.* Prophets were anointed *to a certain people.*

Anointing was never generic. It was always for *something.*

When we separate the oil from the assignment, we end up with priests trying to be kings, kings trying to be prophets, and prophets exhausting themselves trying to do the work of all three. The anointing may be real. The application is wrong.

Anointing is a gift from God. It empowers, quickens, and equips. It allows a person to function beyond natural ability. But anointing alone does not define where that ability is meant to be applied.

Assignment does.

Many discover anointing before they understand assignment. They sense ability, grace, or spiritual effectiveness and assume that wherever they are effective must be where they are meant to remain. But Scripture shows that God often anoints broadly while assigning specifically.

David was anointed king long before he was assigned the throne.

Joseph was gifted with interpretation long before he was assigned authority.

Jesus operated in power yet repeatedly withdrew until the appointed time.

Anointing without assignment creates drift.

When assignment is unclear, anointing is applied wherever opportunity presents itself. Invitations multiply. Needs appear endless. Expectations grow. The person becomes busy—but not necessarily aligned.

This is where burnout begins.

Anointing can sustain output for a season. Assignment sustains obedience for a lifetime. When the two are misaligned, effort increases while peace diminishes.

If the wilderness were rightly understood, it would be valued rather than resisted.

It is not a punishment, but a place of formation. A space where motives are revealed, dependence is learned, and roots are allowed to deepen without the pressure to perform.

The Hebrew word for *wilderness* is *midbar* (מִדְבָּר, Strong's H4057). And here is what is striking about that word: it shares its root with *davar* (דָּבָר, Strong's H1697)—meaning *word* or *to speak*. The Hebrew mind heard *midbar* and heard *the place where God speaks*. The wilderness was not silence. It was the location of the voice.

It is no accident that Israel met God at Sinai in the *midbar*. That John prepared the way in the *midbar*. That Jesus was led by the Spirit into the *midbar* before His ministry began.

Many rush through this season frustrated, complaining about delay—unaware that what feels like waiting is often where God is doing His most careful speaking.

Assignment carries boundaries.

It defines not only what you do, but what you refuse. It limits access. It narrows focus. It clarifies when to say yes—and when to walk away without explanation.

Anointing alone does not provide these limits.

This is why some feel constantly pulled. They respond to every request because they are able, not because they are called. They confuse usefulness with obedience. Over time, the weight of misplaced responsibility erodes clarity.

Assignment brings rest.

When a person knows their assignment, they are no longer tempted to prove anointing through overextension. They no longer feel responsible for outcomes outside their scope. They trust that what is meant for them will align naturally.

Anointing attracts attention. Assignment attracts alignment.

Another danger of confusing anointing with assignment is comparison.

When people evaluate their calling by what others are doing with similar gifts, they begin measuring success incorrectly. They try to replicate impact rather than obey instruction. The uniqueness of assignment is lost in the pursuit of relevance.

Assignment is rarely loud.

It is often confirmed quietly through consistency, peace, and endurance rather than through applause. It does not require constant affirmation to remain compelling. It is sustained by obedience, not reaction.

Anointing can open doors that assignment has not authorized.

Just because a door opens does not mean it should be entered. Opportunity is not permission. Access is not direction. Discernment is required to tell the difference.

When anointing and assignment align, work becomes sustainable. Energy is replenished rather than drained. Clarity replaces striving. The person is no longer driven by demand but directed by purpose.

If you feel effective but unsettled, useful but restless, gifted but fatigued, it may not be a lack of anointing. It may be a misalignment of assignment.

Anointing empowers you to act. Assignment tells you where to stand.

There is a moment in 1 Kings that has stayed with prophets ever since.

Elijah, exhausted after Carmel, ran for his life from Jezebel and collapsed under a juniper tree in the wilderness. He asked to die. He said, *I have had enough, Lord.*

And God did not rebuke him. God did not lecture him on his anointing. God did not remind him of his calling.

God let him sleep. Then sent an angel with bread and water. Then let him sleep again. Then fed him again. Only then did God send him on the long walk to Horeb.

When Elijah finally stood at the cave, God did not appear in the wind, the earthquake, or the fire. God appeared in *qol demamah daqah* (קוֹל דְּמָמָה דַקָּה)—a *thin, still, small voice.*

Anointing burns. Assignment whispers.

If you are exhausted in the place you thought was your assignment, listen for the *qol demamah daqah.* The voice that does not shout. The voice that asks, gently, *What are you doing here?*— to relocate without accusation.

Chapter Eight

Borrowed Fire and Sustained Oil

Fire is immediate.

Oil is cultivated.

Fire draws attention quickly. Oil sustains light quietly. Both can appear powerful, but they are not interchangeable.

Borrowed fire produces instant intensity. It creates urgency, emotion, and movement. It can energize a room, inspire action, and generate response. But fire that is not continually fed will burn out as quickly as it ignites.

Oil behaves differently.

Oil is stored. It is accumulated slowly. It is preserved for use over time. Its strength is not measured by how brightly it flares, but by how consistently it burns.

This distinction matters.

Borrowed fire often comes from proximity rather than preparation. It is ignited by association, atmosphere, or imitation. It borrows language, posture, and urgency from another source without having endured the same process that produced it.

Scripture tells the story of two sons of Aaron who illustrate this exact danger. Nadab and Abihu took their censers and offered *strange fire* before the Lord, fire which He had not commanded them. The Hebrew phrase is *esh zarah* (אֵשׁ זָרָה)—literally *foreign fire*, fire that did not originate from the altar God had ordained. They were priests.

They were anointed. They were positioned. But the fire they brought was borrowed, not begotten.

And the same fire of God that consumed the sacrifice consumed them.

Leviticus does not give us a long explanation. The text simply says fire went out from before the Lord and devoured them. The lesson is older than the church and older than the temple: God does not always burn what is *bad*. Sometimes He burns what is *unauthorized*—because the cost of letting borrowed fire pass for holy fire is greater than the cost of correcting it.

At first, the difference between borrowed fire and holy fire is difficult to detect.

Borrowed fire can look convincing.

It can feel powerful.

It can even produce short-term results.

But it lacks endurance.

When pressure increases, when attention shifts, when affirmation fades, borrowed fire struggles to remain lit. It depends on constant stimulation to survive. Without reinforcement, it cools quickly.

Sustained oil does not require constant ignition.

It burns steadily, even in quiet places. It does not need crowds to function or urgency to feel relevant. It carries light through long nights, not just brief moments of intensity.

This is why Scripture emphasizes oil over fire when speaking of readiness.

The parable of the ten virgins in Matthew 25 turns on a single detail: who had oil, and who did not. All ten had lamps. All ten were waiting. All ten heard the cry at midnight. The difference was not in their position—it was in their preparation. Five had taken time, in unhurried obedience, to fill their flasks. Five had not.

And when the Bridegroom came, the lamps without oil could not be relit by borrowing.

The Greek word for *oil* in that parable is *elaion* (Strong's G1637). In the Hebraic worldview Jesus was speaking from, oil represented the Holy Spirit—the *Ruach HaKodesh*—the slow-pressed, costly, golden weight that came only from olives that had been crushed in the press. There was no shortcut to oil. It came from olives, and olives came from trees, and trees came from years.

Oil must be tended. It must be gathered intentionally. It must be stored with care. This requires foresight, patience, and discipline—qualities that are formed, not assumed.

Borrowed fire avoids this work.

It relies on momentum instead of preparation. It substitutes enthusiasm for endurance. It confuses stimulation with substance.

The danger is not passion. Passion is not the problem.

The danger is mistaking emotional heat for lasting power.

Sustained oil is produced through faithfulness over time. Through obedience when nothing is visible. Through consistency when excitement fades. It is developed in seasons that feel ordinary, repetitive, or even unnoticed.

But oil carries something fire cannot: reliability.

Those who are formed by sustained oil are not destabilized by quiet seasons. They do not panic when intensity lowers. They do not need constant activation to remain effective.

They are steady.

Borrowed fire demands renewal from external sources. Sustained oil is replenished internally through discipline, devotion, and obedience.

This is why some burn out quickly while others endure.

The question is not whether something burns brightly, but whether it can remain lit when conditions are no longer ideal.

Borrowed fire impresses.

Sustained oil remains.

If your growth feels dependent on constant intensity, return to the work of cultivating oil. What is sustained will not need to be reignited every season.

The light that lasts is the light that was prepared for waiting.

There is a small phrase in the Greek of Matthew 25 that is easy to miss.

When the wise virgins were asked to share their oil, they answered: *No, there will not be enough for us and you too; go instead to the dealers and buy some for yourselves* (Matthew 25:9).

On first reading this can feel ungenerous. But the wise virgins were not being unkind. They were being *honest* about something many would not say: oil cannot be shared.

You cannot give another person the years of obedience God has worked into you. You cannot transfer your hidden formation. You cannot pour your *Ruach*-cultivated reserves into someone who has not made room to carry them.

Each person must gather their own oil.

This is not selfishness. It is the unalterable law of formation. The oil is yours because the years were yours. And no shortcut—no proximity, no association, no last-minute borrowing—can manufacture in a moment what the Spirit produces only over time.

Chapter Nine

Image, Influence, and Immaturity

Image grows faster than maturity.

It can be curated, refined, and projected long before character is settled. In a culture shaped by visibility, image often becomes the substitute for formation. What is seen is trusted. What is presented is assumed to be true.

Influence then follows image.

When an image is compelling, people gather. Attention increases. Platforms expand. Influence begins to form—sometimes before the person carrying it has learned how to steward it.

This is where immaturity becomes dangerous.

Immaturity is not a lack of ability. It is a lack of weight. It has not yet learned restraint. It has not yet developed discernment. It has not yet endured enough pressure to know what should and should not be carried.

The Hebrew language has a beautiful word for the kind of weight maturity carries. *Kavod* (כָּבוֹד, Strong's H3519). Most often translated *glory*, but its root meaning is *heaviness, weightiness, substance*. When the *kavod* of God filled the Tabernacle, the priests could not stand. Not because the glory was loud, but because it was *heavy*.

Maturity is *kavod*—weight a person carries that does not need to be announced. You feel it before you hear it. You sense it before they speak.

Image, by contrast, is *qal* (קַל, Strong's H7043)—light, easily lifted, easily moved. Image rides the surface. *Kavod* settles to the bottom.

When influence arrives before maturity, image becomes armor.

Rather than allowing growth to continue inwardly, the person begins protecting how they are perceived. Feedback feels threatening. Correction feels invasive. Silence feels like rejection. The need to maintain appearance begins to shape decisions more than obedience does.

This is subtle, but costly.

Influence magnifies whatever is unresolved. If insecurity remains, it will be amplified. If pride is unchecked, it will be reinforced. If boundaries are unclear, access will be mismanaged.

Image-driven influence requires constant maintenance.

It must be fed. It must be protected. It must be reinforced through repetition and response. The person becomes responsible not only for their work, but for sustaining perception.

This is exhausting.

Mature influence behaves differently.

It does not depend on constant visibility. It does not panic when attention shifts. It is not threatened by quiet seasons. Mature influence understands that credibility is built over time, not managed moment by moment.

Maturity allows image to remain secondary.

When formation has done its work, a person no longer needs to control how they are seen. They are willing to be misunderstood. They are able to be corrected. They can withstand seasons of obscurity without rebranding themselves to regain relevance.

Immaturity resists this.

It looks for shortcuts. It borrows language that has not yet been lived. It imitates posture without understanding process. It wants the outcome without the cost.

This is how fruit appears without roots.

Influence gained too quickly often lacks the structure to sustain responsibility. It can wound others unintentionally. It can create confusion rather than clarity. It can elevate voice without refining wisdom.

This is why God often restricts influence.

Not because He withholds good things, but because He protects people from carrying weight they are not yet formed to bear. Influence entrusted too early becomes a burden rather than a blessing.

Mature influence grows quietly.

It expands in proportion to capacity. It increases as discernment deepens. It carries responsibility with care rather than urgency.

When image is no longer the focus, influence becomes safer.

If you feel pressure to maintain appearance, it may be time to return to formation. What is rooted deeply does not need constant reinforcement. What is mature can wait to be seen.

Image fades.

Influence shifts.

Formation remains.

Scripture gives us two kings to compare on this exact point.

Saul was a man of remarkable image. He stood a head taller than every other man in Israel (1 Samuel 9:2). He looked like what a king should look like. The people *saw* him and wanted him. He was, by every visible measure, the obvious choice.

David was the opposite. When Samuel came to anoint a king from among Jesse's sons, David was not even called in from the field. His own father did not consider him a candidate. When he finally arrived, the Lord had to instruct Samuel directly: *Do not look at his appearance or at the height of his stature… for God sees not as man sees, for man looks at the outward appearance, but the Lord looks at the heart* (1 Samuel 16:7).

The Hebrew word for *heart* is *lev* (לֵב, Strong's H3820). In Hebrew thought, the *lev* was not the seat of emotion the way the modern English word *heart* suggests. The *lev* was the seat of will, decision, character, and inner life. It was the place where a person was actually built.

God did not reject Saul for what he looked like.

God rejected Saul for what his *lev* did not contain.

And here is the warning of that story for every leader: image will get you anointed. Only a formed *lev* will let you finish.

Saul started with everything visible.

He ended hiding among the baggage, consulting a witch, falling on his own sword.

David started with nothing visible.

He ended on the throne, with a covenant that reached forward through Solomon, through Hezekiah, through Josiah, all the way to Bethlehem and the Branch who came from his root.

Image fades.

Lev endures.

And what God is doing in your inner life right now—quietly, slowly, often without your full awareness—is the deepest gift He has given you.

Chapter Ten

When Fruit Attracts Applause but Not Obedience

Applause is easy to confuse with affirmation.

It sounds similar. It feels validating. It suggests approval. But applause responds to what is impressive, not necessarily to what is obedient. It reacts to outcome, not to origin.

Obedience does not always draw applause.

Often it does the opposite.

When fruit attracts applause without producing obedience, something is misaligned. The fruit may look good, but it is not leading people toward transformation. It is admired, discussed, and shared—but not followed.

This is a warning sign.

True fruit carries direction. It does not simply gather attention; it invites response. It does not exist for observation alone. It calls for alignment, change, or commitment. When fruit is God-grown, it produces movement toward truth, not just admiration of it.

The Hebrew concept of obedience is captured in the word *shema* (שָׁמַע, Strong's H8085). It is the famous opening of the Jewish daily prayer: *Shema Yisrael—Hear, O Israel*. But *shema* does not mean *to listen passively*. It means *to hear and to do*. In Hebraic thought, you cannot truly hear without responding. If your life has not changed, you did not actually hear.

This is why James writes that we are to be *doers of the word, and not hearers only, deceiving ourselves* (James 1:22).

He was not introducing a new principle.

He was rebuking a generation that had forgotten *shema*.

Applause allows distance.

A person can applaud without engaging. They can affirm without adjusting. They can celebrate something while remaining unchanged by it. Applause costs little. Obedience costs everything.

This is why applause can be deceptive.

When response is loud but shallow, it creates the illusion of impact. Numbers increase. Feedback multiplies. Momentum builds. But beneath the noise, little is actually shifting. Lives are not being reordered. Patterns are not being confronted. Obedience is not increasing.

The fruit looks healthy, but it is not reproducing in depth.

This kind of fruit often thrives in environments that value reaction over reflection. It is consumed quickly and forgotten just as fast. It moves people emotionally without anchoring them spiritually.

Obedience requires time.

It requires surrender. It requires discomfort. It often requires slowing down rather than speeding up. This is why fruit that leads to obedience does not always spread rapidly. It asks something of the listener. It interrupts patterns rather than reinforcing them.

Applause, on the other hand, asks nothing.

This distinction matters most for those carrying influence.

When applause becomes the metric, content begins to shift. Language is softened. Edges are removed. Messages are shaped to retain response rather than to preserve truth. What began as obedience slowly becomes performance.

This does not happen all at once.

It happens incrementally—one adjustment at a time—until obedience becomes optional and applause becomes necessary.

Fruit that leads to obedience will not always be widely celebrated. It may narrow audience rather than expand it. It may produce fewer responses but deeper ones. It may create silence where noise once existed.

That silence is not failure.

It is often the sound of truth settling.

The Hebrew word for that kind of holy quiet is *demamah* (דְּמָמָה, Strong's H1827)—the *still small voice* Elijah heard at Horeb after the wind, the earthquake, and the fire. God was not in the noise. God was in the *demamah*. The silence was not absence. The silence was where He was speaking.

If fruit consistently attracts attention without producing obedience, it should be examined—not defended. The goal is not to silence applause, but to ensure it is not mistaken for alignment.

Obedience is the truest indicator of health.

Fruit that remains does not need constant reinforcement. It does not depend on reaction to feel valid. It continues to lead people toward truth even when applause fades.

When fruit is rooted in obedience, it does not fear quiet seasons. It knows that transformation often happens slowly, privately, and without recognition.

Applause passes.

Obedience remains.

The crowd that shouted *Hosanna* on Sunday shouted *Crucify* by Friday.

Less than a week separated the two. The same lungs. The same voices. The same throats now demanding what days earlier they had celebrated.

Jesus did not change between Sunday and Friday. The crowd did. Their applause was never about Him. It was about what they wanted Him to do. When He did not become the political deliverer they had imagined, the applause turned to demand, then to fury, then to a verdict.

This is the nature of applause that is not anchored in obedience. It is loud while expectations are met and silent—or hostile—the moment they are not.

If you are leading anything, you will eventually disappoint the crowd. The only question is whether you will be standing on applause when that day comes, or on the rock that does not move when human approval shifts.

Chapter Eleven

Why Some Growth Cannot Be Trusted

Not all growth is healthy.

Growth can be fast, visible, and impressive—and still be unstable. It can expand outward without being strengthened inward. When this happens, growth becomes something to manage rather than something to trust.

Trustworthy growth carries weight.

It is consistent rather than volatile. It deepens as it expands. It can withstand pressure without fracturing. When challenged, it does not collapse or become defensive—it reveals what it has been built upon.

Untrustworthy growth reacts.

It depends on momentum to remain convincing. When momentum slows, anxiety increases. When questioned, it deflects. When corrected, it resists. Its stability is conditional, not settled.

This is one of the clearest indicators that growth has outpaced formation.

Jesus told the parable of the sower and warned of seed that fell on rocky ground. *They have no firm root, and so they endure only for a while; then, when affliction or persecution arises because of the word, immediately they fall away* (Mark 4:17).

The Greek word translated *firm root* is *rhiza* (Strong's G4491)—a literal root, the unseen anchor of the plant. Jesus did not say their problem was lack of zeal. The seed sprang up *immediately*. They were the most enthusiastic of all the soils. Their problem was not visibility—it was depth.

Some of the fastest growth in Scripture is also the most quickly wilted.

Growth that cannot be trusted often requires constant protection. It must be explained, justified, or defended. Those carrying it become vigilant about perception. They monitor response closely. They manage image carefully.

Trustworthy growth does not need this.

It is not threatened by scrutiny because it has been tested privately. It does not fear exposure because it has nothing to hide. Its strength does not come from approval, but from alignment.

Another sign of untrustworthy growth is intolerance of restraint.

When boundaries are introduced, it bristles. When pace is slowed, it pushes back. When limits are applied, it interprets them as opposition rather than wisdom. It confuses restriction with resistance.

But healthy growth welcomes boundaries.

Boundaries clarify purpose. They protect sustainability. They allow strength to mature without strain. Growth that cannot tolerate limits will eventually damage what it touches.

Untrustworthy growth also tends to spread responsibility too thin.

It overextends. It says yes too often. It assumes that because something is possible, it is permissible. Over time, this diffusion weakens focus and erodes discernment.

Growth that can be trusted knows what to carry—and what to release.

It does not grasp for every opportunity. It does not confuse expansion with calling. It understands that stewardship requires restraint as much as action.

This is why God sometimes interrupts growth.

Interruption is not opposition. It is examination.

When growth pauses, what remains is revealed. Motivation surfaces. Foundation is tested. What was being sustained by momentum must now stand on formation alone.

Those who are rooted endure interruption without panic.

Those who are not often rush to recreate momentum rather than allowing examination.

Trustworthy growth does not fear slowing down. It recognizes that endurance matters more than acceleration. It understands that what is meant to last must be able to withstand seasons without visible progress.

Growth that cannot be trusted will eventually require control.

Growth that can be trusted produces peace.

If growth in your life feels fragile—easily threatened, easily disrupted—it may not be ready to be expanded further. This is not condemnation. It is discernment.

Some growth is genuine, but premature.

What is trusted has been tested.

And what has been tested does not need to be rushed.

There is no clearer picture in Scripture of growth that cannot be trusted than the tower at Babel.

Come, let us build for ourselves a city, and a tower whose top will reach into heaven, and let us make for ourselves a name (Genesis 11:4).

Read that verse slowly.

Notice what it does not say. It does not say, *Let us seek the Lord.* It does not say, *Let us obey His instruction.* It does not say, *Let us be planted by Him.* It says, *Let us build for ourselves… let us make for ourselves a name.*

The growth at Babel was real. The construction was real. The unity was real. The accomplishment was real. By every metric a modern strategist would use, Babel was working.

And God came down and stopped it.

Not because the people were doing something obviously evil. There is no record of murder, theft, or idolatry being attached to the tower itself. The judgment was not against their behavior. It was against their *direction*.

Babel was growth pointed away from God toward man's own glory.

Let us make for ourselves a name.

The Hebrew word for *name* is *shem* (שֵׁם, Strong's H8034)—which means more than identification. *Shem* in Hebrew thought meant reputation, renown, the weight a person carried in the world. It was identity made public.

There is only one *shem* a man should pursue: the *Shem* of the Lord. The Father is the only one who gives a *shem* that can carry weight without crushing the one who bears it.

When growth is built for *our* name, it cannot be trusted, no matter how impressive it looks.

When growth is built for *His* name, it can be trusted, no matter how slow it appears.

This is one of the most important questions a leader can ask in any season of increase: *Whose name is this growth making?*

If the answer is honestly *His*, the growth is safe.

If the answer is *mine*, the tower is going to come down. Either by God's mercy now, or by time's exposure later.

Chapter Twelve

The Mercy of Closed Doors

Closed doors are often interpreted as loss.

They feel abrupt. Final. Limiting. When a door closes, it interrupts momentum and challenges expectation. It forces a pause where continuation seemed logical. This is why closed doors are often resisted rather than received.

But not all closure is opposition.

Some doors close as an act of mercy.

A closed door can prevent misalignment before it becomes damage. It can stop growth from moving into a space it is not yet formed to sustain. It can shield a person from carrying responsibility that would exhaust rather than establish them.

1 Corinthians 3:10–11

"According to the grace of God which was given to me, like a wise master builder I laid a foundation, and another is building on it. But each man must be careful how he builds on it. For no man can lay a foundation other than the one which is laid, which is Jesus Christ."

The Greek word for *foundation* is *themelios* (Strong's G2310). It is not the visible part of a building. It is the buried portion, the part no inspector sees once construction is complete. And yet it is the part that determines whether the structure stands or falls.

Closed doors are often the work of the Master Builder strengthening a foundation that the builder himself could not yet see needed to be deepened.

Mercy does not always feel gentle.

Sometimes it feels like restriction. Sometimes it feels like disappointment. Sometimes it feels like being passed over or left out. But mercy is not measured by comfort—it is measured by outcome.

The Hebrew word for *mercy* is *chesed* (חֶסֶד, Strong's H2617)—a word so rich the English language has no single equivalent. It carries the meaning of *covenant loyalty, faithful kindness, lovingkindness that does not break*. It is the love of a covenant-keeping Father who knows what His child cannot yet see.

Chesed sometimes opens doors.

Chesed sometimes closes them.

Both are love.

Closed doors protect assignment.

They prevent diffusion. They narrow focus. They clarify direction by removing alternatives that look appealing but would ultimately divide attention. When too many doors remain open, discernment weakens. Energy spreads thin. Purpose becomes diluted.

A closed door brings clarity.

It removes the pressure to decide. It ends negotiation. It settles questions that would otherwise linger. While this can feel abrupt, it often produces peace once the initial resistance subsides.

This is why some doors close without explanation.

Explanation invites debate. Closure invites trust.

God does not always clarify why a door has closed because understanding is not always necessary for obedience. What matters is whether the closure redirects you toward alignment or pulls you into striving.

Merciful closure often reveals itself over time.

What initially felt like loss becomes protection. What seemed like delay becomes preservation. What appeared to be rejection becomes redirection. In hindsight, the door that closed often prevented harm that was not visible at the time.

Closed doors also test attachment.

They reveal whether identity has become entangled with opportunity. When a door closes, what remains exposed is not the loss of access, but the reaction to it. If peace disappears with opportunity, something has been misplaced.

Stewardship requires acceptance of limits.

A person who cannot accept closed doors will continually force openings that were never authorized. They will equate persistence with faith and pressure with obedience. Over time, this creates fatigue and confusion rather than fruit.

Closed doors are not the absence of favor.

They are often evidence of it.

When God closes a door, He is not reducing capacity—He is refining direction. He is narrowing focus so that what remains can be carried well. He is protecting what has been formed from being misapplied.

Receiving a closed door with humility preserves strength.

Resisting it drains energy.

Mercy does not always look like expansion. Sometimes it looks like restraint. Sometimes it looks like limitation. Sometimes it looks like being told no.

But restraint now prevents regret later.

What God closes, He closes with intention.

And what is closed by mercy does not need to be reopened by force.

There is a beautiful Hebrew word that runs through the closing chapters of Genesis: *zakar* (זָכַר, Strong's H2142)—*to remember. God remembered Noah* (Genesis 8:1). *God remembered Abraham* (Genesis 19:29). *God remembered Rachel* (Genesis 30:22). Each time the word *zakar* appears, the story is about to turn.

Zakar in the Hebrew mind was not the recovery of forgotten information. God had not actually forgotten anyone. *Zakar* was *to act on behalf of*. To bring forward into the present what had been quietly held. To open a door that, until that moment, had appeared closed.

When God closes a door, He has not stopped *zakar*ing you. The closure is part of the remembering. He is holding you, and your assignment, and the timing, and the next door, all at once. What looks like rejection is often Him rearranging the architecture of the season so that the door He opens next will be the one your formation can carry.

When Teaching Becomes Governance

Teaching informs.

Governance establishes.

In early seasons, teaching is primarily invitational. It offers insight, perspective, and understanding. It opens doors rather than closing them. It explains rather than restricts. Its goal is illumination.

But there comes a point when teaching shifts.

It stops merely informing and begins governing.

This transition is subtle, and often misunderstood. When teaching becomes governance, it no longer exists only to communicate truth—it exists to order life. It carries boundaries. It clarifies responsibility. It establishes what is permitted and what is not.

Not everyone is comfortable with this shift.

Governance removes ambiguity.

It does not ask, *What do you think?*

It asks, *What will you do?*

This is why governance often reduces audience even as it increases authority. Those who were content to listen disengage when obedience is implied. Those who enjoyed reflection resist when instruction requires alignment.

Teaching that governs is no longer neutral.

It carries weight.

The Hebrew word *torah* (תּוֹרָה, Strong's H8451) is most often translated *law*, but its primary meaning is *instruction* or *teaching*. Yet *torah* was never abstract instruction in the Hebrew mind. *Torah* was instruction *that ordered life*. It told you when to plant, when to rest, when to gather, when to give, when to draw near, when to step back. It was teaching that became governance.

The root of *torah* is *yarah* (יָרָה, Strong's H3384)—meaning *to throw, to shoot an arrow, to direct, to point the way*. Real teaching is directional. It does not float. It aims.

This is why Jesus' words often divided listeners. He did not only explain truth—He embodied it, and then required response. His teaching reordered priorities, challenged assumptions, and disrupted patterns. It was not merely informative; it was formative.

Governance introduces consequence.

It clarifies what is at stake. It draws lines. It establishes order where preference once ruled. This can feel restrictive to those accustomed to choice without cost.

But governance is necessary for maturity.

A life without governance drifts. A community without governance fractures. Influence without governance becomes unstable. Teaching that never governs leaves people informed but unanchored.

Governance also requires restraint from the one carrying it.

When teaching becomes governance, the teacher no longer speaks casually. Words are weighed. Timing matters. Silence becomes as important as speech. Not every thought is shared. Not every insight is released.

This is stewardship.

Governance understands that words create pathways. Once spoken, they shape behavior. Once established, they carry responsibility. This is why mature teachers do not rush to speak—they recognize the authority their words now hold.

This shift often feels lonely.

When teaching governed lightly, affirmation was frequent. When teaching begins to govern, resistance increases. Questions become sharper. Motives are examined. Alignment is tested.

This is not failure.

It is confirmation that the teaching has weight.

Governance does not aim to be liked. It aims to be trusted. It does not seek consensus. It establishes order. Those who are ready recognize it immediately. Those who are not often withdraw quietly.

This separation is not punitive.

It is protective.

Teaching that governs creates stability for those who submit to it. It provides clarity, direction, and safety. It removes confusion. It defines expectation.

But governance is never imposed.

It is received.

Those who resist governance are not rejected—they are simply not aligned with that level of responsibility. Teaching continues to exist, but access changes. Authority narrows. Depth increases.

This is why governance always follows formation.

Without formation, governance becomes control. Without humility, it becomes domination. But when carried by someone who has been formed in hidden places, governance becomes a gift.

It provides structure for growth.

It protects what has been planted.

It ensures that fruit remains.

When teaching becomes governance, it is no longer about sharing insight.

It is about stewarding life.

The Sermon on the Mount is the clearest example in Scripture of teaching that became governance.

When Jesus finished speaking, *the crowds were amazed at His teaching; for He was teaching them as one having authority, and not as their scribes* (Matthew 7:28–29).

The Greek word for *authority* there is *exousia* (Strong's G1849)— a word that means *the right to act, derived from the source.* The scribes had information. They had knowledge. They had memorized texts. But they did not have *exousia.* They could explain Torah. They could not embody it.

Jesus did both.

And His teaching, because it carried *exousia*, did not merely inform the crowd—it ordered their lives. The Beatitudes were not nine pleasant sayings. They were a re-ranking of every value the world held. *Blessed are the poor in spirit* upended success. *Blessed are those who mourn* upended pleasure. *Blessed are the meek* upended power.

When Jesus finished, the world's order had been challenged at its root.

That is what teaching does when it becomes governance. It does not give you new information to add to your existing life. It gives you a new life that reorders everything else.

This is why governance always meets resistance.

Information is welcome. New facts feel like a gift. But governance asks you to lay something down. It asks you to change. It asks you to align. And the soul that has not yet been broken to the will of God will always resist that invitation, no matter how kindly it is offered.

The teacher who governs is not unkind. They are simply *true*.

And truth, fully spoken, has always cost both the speaker and the listener something.

Chapter Fourteen

Saying No Without Explaining

Early on, *no* feels like something that must be justified.

It is accompanied by reasons, context, and reassurance. We explain our limits to soften disappointment. We defend our boundaries to avoid misunderstanding. We clarify our decisions so they will be accepted.

This is common in formative seasons.

But as stewardship matures, something changes.

No no longer requires explanation.

Not because explanation is wrong, but because authority has settled. When a person is clear about their assignment, they are no longer compelled to negotiate it. They trust the alignment enough to allow misunderstanding without correction.

This is a mark of maturity.

Saying no without explaining is not dismissive. It is decisive. It signals that discernment has already taken place internally and does not need external validation to be legitimate.

Explanation invites debate.

Clarity does not.

When explanations are given too freely, boundaries become porous. Each justification opens the door for negotiation. Each clarification invites reconsideration. Over time, what was meant to protect focus begins to erode it.

This is exhausting.

Mature stewardship recognizes that not every no is owed an explanation. Some decisions are directional, not relational. They are about obedience, not preference. They are rooted in responsibility, not reaction.

Jesus modeled this restraint.

He did not respond to every demand. He did not heal every person who asked. He did not explain every decision to those who followed Him. At times, He withdrew without announcement. At other times, He answered questions with silence.

When the Pharisees asked Him by what authority He was teaching, He answered with a question of His own and refused to satisfy their demand. When Herod questioned Him, *He gave him no answer* (Luke 23:9). When Pilate demanded a defense, *Jesus made no further answer* (Mark 15:5).

This was not avoidance.

It was discernment.

There is a Hebrew principle called *shomer*—to *guard, to keep, to watch over.* The word is the root of *shomer Shabbat* (one who keeps the Sabbath) and *shomer mitzvot* (one who keeps the commandments). A *shomer* understands that keeping requires *not letting in.* The watchman does not explain to every traveler at the gate why he cannot pass. He guards. He decides. He keeps.

Saying no without explaining is the work of a *shomer* over your own assignment.

Saying no without explaining requires confidence that obedience does not require consensus. It trusts that those who are aligned will understand—or will not need to. It also trusts that misunderstanding does not threaten assignment.

This is difficult for those who are still shaped by approval.

If affirmation is still required, explanation becomes a tool to preserve it. Boundaries are softened to maintain connection. Decisions are delayed to avoid disappointment. *No* becomes conditional.

But stewardship cannot function this way.

Stewardship demands decisiveness.

It recognizes that clarity will disappoint some and protect others. It accepts that saying no may close doors that will not reopen. It understands that not every relationship is meant to accompany every season.

This is not unkind.

It is ordered.

Those who are meant to walk with you in a particular assignment will not require extensive explanation. They will recognize alignment when they see it. Those who demand justification often do so because their expectations are no longer being met.

Saying no without explaining is an act of trust.

It trusts that God can manage perception.

It trusts that alignment will reveal itself over time.

It trusts that obedience is sufficient.

This does not mean becoming inaccessible or unresponsive. It means becoming clear. It means allowing decisions to stand without defense. It means resisting the urge to over-communicate when silence would preserve peace.

Boundaries held quietly are often the strongest.

If you find yourself explaining no repeatedly, it may be time to examine why. Stewardship is not strengthened by constant reassurance. It is strengthened by consistency.

No spoken with clarity creates space for what matters most.

And what is protected by restraint will be sustained.

Even in His final hours, Jesus chose silence over explanation.

Pilate asked, *Are You the King of the Jews?* He answered briefly. Pilate asked again. He answered with a question. Pilate asked, *Where are You from?* He gave him no answer. Mark records simply: *Jesus made no further answer; so Pilate was amazed* (Mark 15:5).

The Greek word for *amazed* is *thaumazō* (Strong's G2296)—to be astonished, to marvel. Pilate had interrogated countless prisoners. He had never met one who refused to defend himself.

Jesus did not need to defend Himself because He was not on trial. The kingdom was on trial. And the kingdom does not negotiate.

Chapter Fifteen

Why Depth Repels the Unformed

Depth is not neutral.

It attracts some and repels others—not because it is unkind, but because it requires something in return. Depth asks for attention, patience, and surrender. It cannot be skimmed without consequence.

Those who are unformed often sense this immediately.

Depth slows the pace.

It removes shortcuts.

It exposes what has not yet been settled.

This is why depth can feel uncomfortable to those who prefer momentum over maturity.

The unformed are often drawn to environments where growth is fast and affirmation is frequent. They prefer spaces where response is immediate and expectations are minimal. Depth disrupts this rhythm. It introduces silence. It requires listening rather than reacting.

Matthew 7:6

"Do not give what is holy to dogs, and do not throw your pearls before swine, or they will trample them under their feet, and turn and tear you to pieces."

This is one of the more uncomfortable verses in the Sermon on the Mount, but it is consistent with everything Jesus teaches about formation. He did not entrust Himself to all who believed (John

2:24). He withdrew from crowds. He spoke in parables specifically so that those without ears to hear would not be given more than they could carry.

The Hebrew word *amok* (עָמֹק, Strong's H6013) means *deep, profound, unsearchable*. It is the word used for *deep waters*, for the *deep things of God*, for wisdom that requires diving rather than wading. The Hebraic mind associated *amok* with reverence. You did not splash in deep water. You approached it slowly, carefully, with awareness that depth had its own dignity.

Depth refuses to entertain.

It does not adjust itself to maintain interest. It does not simplify itself to broaden appeal. It does not rush conclusions to keep attention. Instead, it holds its ground and allows the listener to decide whether they will stay.

This is where separation occurs.

Those who are ready lean in.

Those who are not often drift away quietly.

This drifting is not rejection—it is discernment at work. Depth naturally filters without force. It reveals readiness without confrontation. It creates space for those who are prepared while releasing those who are not.

The unformed often interpret this as exclusion.

They assume depth is elitist or inaccessible. But depth is not reserved for a few—it is available to anyone willing to slow down. What feels like exclusion is often resistance to the cost.

Depth demands consistency.

It asks for faithfulness over time rather than intensity in moments. It rewards endurance rather than novelty. For those who have learned to rely on excitement or urgency, this can feel unsatisfying.

Depth does not reward impatience.

It reveals patterns rather than producing spectacle. It exposes motives rather than amplifying emotion. It confronts what has been avoided rather than affirming what is comfortable.

This is why depth cannot be marketed effectively.

It does not translate well into soundbites. It cannot be reduced without losing integrity. It resists being packaged for mass consumption because it was never designed for that purpose.

Depth is relational.

It requires trust. It develops over time. It deepens through consistency and shared experience. Those who are unformed often prefer transactional environments—spaces where engagement is optional and cost is low.

Depth refuses transaction.

It asks for presence. It requires commitment. It invites transformation rather than observation.

This is not harsh.

It is honest.

Depth protects both the message and the listener. It prevents premature engagement that would produce frustration rather than growth. It ensures that what is received can be sustained.

Those who are repelled by depth are not being rejected.

They are being spared.

What they are not yet formed to carry would become a burden. What they are not ready to receive would create confusion. Depth waits until capacity catches up with desire.

For those who remain, depth becomes a place of stability.

It anchors identity.

It sharpens discernment.

It produces fruit that does not fade quickly.

Depth does not chase attention.

It remains.

And what remains continues to shape long after others have moved on.

There is a moment in John 6 that captures this exactly.

Jesus had just fed the five thousand. The crowds were enormous. He was at the height of His earthly popularity. They had even tried to take Him by force and make Him king.

And then He began to teach.

Truly, truly, I say to you, unless you eat the flesh of the Son of Man and drink His blood, you have no life in yourselves (John 6:53).

It was a hard saying. It was meant to be. He was speaking in the deepest possible Hebraic imagery—of covenant, of identification, of total dependence on Him as both Bread and Lamb. But the crowd was not listening for depth. They had come for bread.

John records what happened next: *As a result of this many of His disciples withdrew and were not walking with Him anymore* (John 6:66).

Notice the word *disciples.*

These were not casual onlookers. These were people who had been following Him—who had given Him their time, their attention, their public association. And one teaching of sufficient depth was enough to send them back to wherever they came from.

Then Jesus turned to the Twelve.

You do not want to go away also, do you?

Peter answered: *Lord, to whom shall we go? You have words of eternal life.*

That is the answer of the formed heart.

Not, *I understood every word.* Not, *I am comfortable with this teaching.* Not even, *This makes sense to me.* Just: *Where else would I go?*

Depth does this work in every generation.

It does not always feel kind in the moment. It rarely produces the largest crowd. It will, with quiet certainty, do what Jesus did at Capernaum: thin the gathering until what remains is the gathering that was always meant to remain.

Do not be alarmed when this happens around your own teaching. It is the Master's pattern.

Chapter Sixteen

Letting God Do the Separating

Separation is inevitable.

Not everyone who begins with you is meant to continue with you. Not every connection is designed to last through every season. As growth deepens and assignment clarifies, alignment becomes more specific.

This is not failure.

It is order.

When separation is forced by human effort, it creates strain. It produces offense, defensiveness, and unnecessary conflict. But when separation is entrusted to God, it unfolds quietly and without damage.

Letting God do the separating requires restraint.

It resists the urge to confront prematurely. It avoids explanations that are not required. It refuses to manage outcomes that obedience will naturally resolve. It trusts that alignment will reveal itself without intervention.

This kind of trust is difficult.

We often feel responsible for clarifying roles, correcting misunderstanding, or maintaining connection. But not all distance requires explanation. Some relationships loosen simply because the season has changed.

Scripture gives us a clear picture of this in the parting of Abraham and Lot. The land could not support both their flocks. Strife arose between their herdsmen. And Abraham, the older and the more honored, said simply: *Let there be no strife between you and me... if you go to the left, then I will go to the right; or if you go to the right, then I will go to the left* (Genesis 13:8–9).

He did not lecture Lot.

He did not protect his own portion.

He let God do the separating.

And it was *after* Lot departed that the Lord said to Abraham, *Now lift up your eyes and look... for all the land which you see, I will give it to you* (Genesis 13:14–15). The promise was not narrowed by separation. It was unveiled because of it.

God orchestrates this gently.

He shifts priorities. He redirects attention. He introduces new responsibilities. Over time, what once fit no longer aligns. Conversations thin. Proximity changes. What felt necessary becomes optional.

This is not rejection.

It is refinement.

The Hebrew word for *separate* in the creation account is *badal* (בָּדַל, Strong's H914). God *separated* the light from the darkness. He *separated* the waters above from the waters below. He *separated* the dry land from the seas. *Badal* is not a word of rupture. It is a word of *order*. It is the work of distinguishing what belongs in one place from what belongs in another so that life can flourish.

When God *badals* a relationship, He is not destroying it. He is placing each person where they belong.

When God separates, He does so without accusation. He does not shame those who depart. He does not elevate those who remain. He simply allows alignment to take shape according to purpose rather than preference.

This protects everyone involved.

Forced separation wounds.

Divinely ordered separation preserves.

When we intervene unnecessarily, we risk creating fracture where distance would have resolved itself. We turn seasons into statements. We assign motives where timing was sufficient explanation.

Letting God separate keeps the heart clean.

It allows gratitude without attachment. It preserves respect without obligation. It releases control without resentment. Those who leave are blessed—not blamed.

This does not mean avoiding all difficult conversations. It means discerning which conversations are required and which would only satisfy discomfort.

Some separations are not meant to be discussed.

They are meant to be accepted.

God separates by assignment, not by conflict. As calling narrows, access adjusts. As responsibility increases, proximity shifts. This happens naturally when obedience is prioritized over familiarity.

Those who are aligned will remain without effort.

Those who are not will disengage without confrontation.

This is mercy.

Separation handled by God preserves integrity. It prevents entanglement. It protects what is being built without dismantling what has already been shared.

When you trust God with separation, you no longer need to manage relationships to maintain peace. Peace becomes the result of obedience rather than negotiation.

Those who belong will recognize the season.

Those who do not will move on without harm.

Letting God do the separating keeps the work clean and the heart clear.

And what remains after separation is what is meant to be stewarded into the next season.

Paul and Barnabas had a sharp disagreement over John Mark and parted ways (Acts 15:39).

Scripture does not soften this. The Greek word for the disagreement is *paroxysmos* (Strong's G3948)—a sharp, irritating dispute. The same root word from which we get *paroxysm*. They did not part politely. They parted in fire.

And yet—notice what God did with that separation.

Two missionary teams went out instead of one. Paul took Silas and went through Syria and Cilicia. Barnabas took Mark and sailed for Cyprus. The single ministry split into two ministries, and the kingdom advanced in two directions instead of one.

Years later, Paul would write to Timothy: *Pick up Mark and bring him with you, for he is useful to me for service* (2 Timothy 4:11). The very man he had separated from in *paroxysmos* was, by the end, useful again.

God uses separations we would not choose. He multiplies what looks broken. He restores what looks finished. The work of separation, when entrusted to Him, is never wasted. It is rearranged.

Chapter Seventeen

Fruit That Remains

Not all fruit is meant to last.

Some fruit serves a moment. It meets a need, answers a question, or marks a season. It appears, fulfills its purpose, and passes away without failure. But Scripture speaks of a different kind of fruit—fruit that remains.

John 15:16

"You did not choose Me but I chose you, and appointed you that you would go and bear fruit, and that your fruit would remain."

The Greek word translated *remain* is *menō* (Strong's G3306)—the same word translated *abide* in the verses just before. *Bear fruit… that your fruit would abide.*

Jesus uses one word for two realities. The fruit *abides* because the branch *abides*. The fruit *remains* because the source has not been broken. There is no fruit that *remains* apart from a relationship that *remains*. The two are inseparable in the Greek as they are inseparable in life.

Remaining fruit is not measured by longevity alone.

It is measured by impact that continues after visibility fades.

Fruit that remains is rooted in obedience, not momentum. It is sustained by alignment rather than activity. It does not depend on constant reinforcement to stay relevant. Its value is not diminished by time or obscurity.

This kind of fruit grows slowly.

It is formed through faithfulness over long periods, often without recognition. It develops depth before it develops reach. By the time it is visible, it has already endured seasons that tested its integrity.

Remaining fruit carries substance.

It changes lives quietly. It reshapes patterns over time. It produces transformation that cannot be traced to a single moment or message, but to consistent truth applied patiently.

This is why remaining fruit is often underestimated.

It does not announce itself. It does not demand attention. It continues working beneath the surface long after interest has moved elsewhere. Those shaped by it may not remember the moment it began—but they live differently because of it.

Remaining fruit is not flashy.

It does not rely on novelty. It does not need to reinvent itself to stay relevant. It carries principles rather than trends. Its strength lies in its ability to be returned to again and again without losing meaning.

This fruit survives seasons of pruning.

Pruning does not threaten it. It strengthens it. What is removed does not diminish what remains—it clarifies it. Remaining fruit understands that reduction is often preparation for longevity.

The Greek word for *prune* in John 15:2 is *kathairō* (Strong's G2508)—meaning *to cleanse, to purify, to make clean by removal.* The vinedresser does not punish a fruitful branch. He cleans it. He cuts away what is sapping its strength so that what remains can bear more.

Pruning is not loss.

Pruning is *kathairō*—the patient cleansing of a branch the Father intends to keep.

Those who pursue remaining fruit are not driven by scale.

They are guided by faithfulness. They are willing to labor without immediate outcome. They trust that what is planted in obedience will surface in its appointed time.

Remaining fruit often outlives its planter.

It continues bearing through others. It multiplies through faithfulness rather than imitation. It leaves a legacy that is not dependent on personality or platform.

This is the fruit Jesus spoke of when He said it would remain.

It is the result of abiding rather than striving. It grows from connection rather than performance. It is sustained by relationship rather than reaction.

If your desire is for fruit that lasts, return again and again to the root.

Remain in truth.

Remain in obedience.

Remain in formation.

What remains is rarely loud—but it is always lasting.

There is a Hebraic concept woven through the Torah called *shevet*—the seventh year. Every seventh year, the land was to rest.

Fields were not to be sown. Vineyards were not to be pruned. The land was to lie fallow, recovering, breathing, deepening.

The harvest of the seventh year was not like the harvests of the first six.

It was not what the farmer had produced.

It was what God Himself had grown while no one was working.

Fruit that remains is often *shevet* fruit. It is what God grew in the season when you were not striving. It is what came up from soil that had been allowed to rest. It is what the Master Himself produced while you were learning, finally, to abide.

Do not overlook *shevet* fruit. It is some of the most enduring fruit you will ever bear.

Chapter Eighteen

Legacy Over Momentum

Momentum is powerful, but it is temporary.

It thrives on speed, reaction, and response. It creates movement quickly and gives the impression of progress. But momentum, by nature, must be maintained. When energy wanes, when attention shifts, when conditions change, momentum slows.

Legacy behaves differently.

Legacy is not dependent on pace. It is not threatened by quiet seasons. It does not require constant reinforcement to remain meaningful. Legacy is built intentionally, with endurance in mind rather than immediacy.

Momentum asks, *How far can this go?*

Legacy asks, *What will remain?*

This distinction changes how decisions are made.

When momentum is the goal, choices prioritize expansion. Opportunities are evaluated by reach. Success is measured by visibility. The pressure to sustain movement becomes central.

When legacy is the goal, choices prioritize integrity. Opportunities are evaluated by alignment. Success is measured by depth and durability rather than speed.

Momentum seeks acceleration.

Legacy requires patience.

There is a Hebrew word that captures the heart of legacy: *zera* (זֶרַע, Strong's H2233)—*seed, offspring, that which is sown for generations to come. Zera* is not what you eat. *Zera* is what you save. It is the portion of the harvest withheld from immediate consumption so that next year's field will not be empty.

A man who eats his *zera* has a full belly today and a barren field tomorrow.

A man who plants his *zera* may go hungry today, but his children will eat for years.

The kingdom is built by people who understand the difference.

Legacy-building often looks inefficient to those focused on growth metrics. It resists shortcuts. It invests in processes that do not yield immediate results. It values consistency over novelty and substance over spectacle.

This can feel countercultural.

In seasons of momentum, restraint can look like hesitation. Boundaries can appear limiting. Silence can be misinterpreted as disengagement. But those committed to legacy understand that not every opportunity strengthens what is meant to last.

Some opportunities dilute focus.

Some invitations distract from assignment.

Some expansions weaken foundation.

Legacy requires discernment to say no—even to good things.

Legacy also requires humility.

It acknowledges that the most significant impact may occur beyond one's lifetime. It resists the urge to control outcomes or secure recognition. It trusts that what is built in obedience will continue bearing fruit without constant oversight.

Momentum wants results now.

Legacy trusts the process.

Those who build for legacy are willing to plant what they may not personally harvest. They invest in people rather than platforms. They establish principles rather than programs. They create structures that can function without their presence.

Abraham died before he saw the nation he was promised. Moses died before he entered the land he had led toward. David died before the Temple he had dreamed of was built. The faithful in Hebrews 11 *all died in faith, without receiving the promises, but having seen them and welcomed them from a distance* (Hebrews 11:13).

They were not failures.

They were *legacy*.

This does not mean avoiding growth.

It means guiding growth with intention.

Momentum without legacy burns bright and fades. Legacy may grow quietly, but it continues shaping long after attention has moved on.

If momentum begins to dictate decisions, pause. Recenter on purpose. Ask whether what is being built can endure without constant maintenance.

What requires constant effort to sustain may not be designed to last.

Legacy grows from roots, not reaction.

Choose legacy over momentum—not because momentum is wrong, but because it is insufficient.

What remains will not be determined by how fast something moved, but by how faithfully it was formed.

There is a phrase in Hebrew that captures the heart of generational legacy: *l'dor v'dor* (לְדֹר וָדֹר)—*from generation to generation.*

It is woven into the Psalms. It is woven into the prayers. It is the long view that the Hebraic mind has always carried in a way the modern Western mind does not.

One generation shall praise Your works to another (Psalm 145:4).

Your faithfulness continues throughout all generations (Psalm 119:90).

Legacy in Scripture is not a personal monument. It is a baton. It is meant to leave your hand.

Build *l'dor v'dor.* Build for hands you may never see hold what you started. That is the kind of building that outlives every generation's applause and every season's noise.

Chapter Nineteen

Teaching That Ages Well

Isaiah 55:11

*"So will My word be which goes forth from My mouth; it will not
return to Me empty, without accomplishing what I desire, and
without succeeding in the matter for which I sent it."*

The Hebrew word for *word* in this passage is *davar* (דָּבָר, Strong's H1697). It is the same root we encountered in chapter seven—the word from which *midbar*, the wilderness, derives. But *davar* itself does not merely mean *word* in the sense of sound. *Davar* means *word, matter, thing, event, that which has been spoken into existence.*

When God *davars* something, He does not just say it. He *creates* it. The word and the thing are inseparable.

This is why Hebrew prophecy did not age the way human speech ages. Because what God spoke was not a description of reality but the *establishment* of reality. The *davar* of the Lord is not commentary. It is creation.

Teaching that ages well participates in this same quality. It is not merely articulate. It is *anchored*. It does not describe the truth from a distance. It carries it.

Time is an uncompromising evaluator.

It does not respond to intention or enthusiasm. It is not persuaded by popularity or defended by explanation. Over time, what is built reveals what it was built on.

Teaching that ages well is not driven by urgency.

It is not reactive. It does not chase relevance or reshape itself to match every cultural shift. It speaks from settled conviction rather than immediate pressure. As a result, it remains useful long after the moment that produced it has passed.

Teaching that does not age well depends on context to survive.

It is tethered to trends, language, or urgency that eventually fades. When conditions change, it loses clarity. When attention moves elsewhere, it becomes obsolete. It may have been effective for a season, but it was not designed for endurance.

Teaching that ages well is anchored.

It returns again and again to first principles. It emphasizes truth that remains stable across time rather than insight that dazzles briefly. It is careful with language, restrained in claims, and deliberate in application.

This kind of teaching does not attempt to say everything.

It says what is necessary.

One of the marks of teaching that ages well is restraint.

It avoids exaggeration. It resists overstatement. It does not inflate impact to generate response. It trusts that truth carries its own authority and does not require embellishment to be compelling.

This restraint protects credibility.

As years pass, the teaching remains accurate. It does not require revision to correct excess. It does not need to be distanced from because of overreach. Those who return to it find clarity rather than discomfort.

Teaching that ages well also respects process.

It acknowledges complexity. It allows room for growth. It does not present transformation as immediate or effortless. It honors the slow work of formation and the varied pace at which people mature.

This makes it durable.

Teaching that promises quick outcomes may gather attention, but it often produces disillusionment over time. Teaching that honors process prepares people for reality. It strengthens them for endurance rather than exciting them for a moment.

Teaching that ages well is not defensive.

It does not require protection from scrutiny. It can withstand questions because it is not built on novelty. It invites examination rather than resisting it. Over time, it proves itself not by volume of response, but by consistency of impact.

This is why teaching that ages well is often quieter.

It does not announce itself loudly. It does not demand to be heard. It simply remains available—ready to be returned to when clarity is needed.

Those who build teaching with longevity in mind are not preoccupied with immediate reception. They understand that time will do what promotion cannot. What is true will endure. What is exaggerated will eventually be exposed.

Teaching that ages well serves multiple generations.

It does not depend on shared context to be understood. It speaks to principles that transcend moment and medium. It remains useful even as circumstances change.

If your desire is to teach in a way that lasts, resist the pressure to impress. Choose clarity over cleverness. Choose truth over urgency. Choose restraint over reach.

What ages well does not require constant updating.

It simply remains.

Consider Solomon.

He was given more wisdom than any man before or since. The kings of the earth came from far countries to hear him speak. He wrote three thousand proverbs and a thousand and five songs (1 Kings 4:32). He spoke about trees, animals, birds, fish—the visible and the invisible.

And yet most of what Solomon said is gone.

We have a fragment—the book of Proverbs, the Song of Songs, Ecclesiastes. Roughly thirty-one chapters of pithy sayings, one love poem, and one searching meditation on vanity. The remaining thousands of his words have not survived.

Why?

Not because they were poorly spoken. Solomon was not a careless speaker. He was the wisest man of his age.

But teaching that endures is not measured by how clever it was when first spoken. It is measured by how *necessary* it remains across generations.

What survived of Solomon was not his cleverness.

What survived was the part of him that was *anchored*—the part that returned again and again to the fear of the Lord, to the brevity of life, to the futility of self-glory.

The fear of the Lord is the beginning of knowledge (Proverbs 1:7).

All is vanity… fear God and keep His commandments (Ecclesiastes 12:8, 13).

These were not his most original lines.

They were his most *rooted* ones.

And it was the rooted ones that lasted.

If you are a teacher—of anything—let this comfort you and warn you in equal measure. The cleverest things you say will not be what your hearers carry. The lines you reach for to gain a response will not be the lines that change a life. What endures is what was rooted before it was spoken.

Chapter Twenty

Who This Is Really For

This book is not for everyone.

That is not a disclaimer meant to sound selective or severe. It is a recognition of alignment. Some writing is meant to invite broadly. Other writing is meant to locate those who are already listening.

This is the latter.

This book is for those who have outgrown spectacle.

For those who no longer confuse movement with maturity.

For those who have felt the tension between visibility and obedience—and chosen restraint.

It is for those who sense when something is impressive but hollow. For those who recognize when growth is happening faster than formation. For those who have felt uneasy applauding fruit that did not require surrender.

This book is for the formed—or for those willing to be.

2 Timothy 2:15

"Be diligent to present yourself approved to God as a workman who does not need to be ashamed, accurately handling the word of truth."

The Greek word translated *accurately handling* is *orthotomeō* (Strong's G3718)—literally *to cut straight*, the word a stonemason would use for a wall built true, or a craftsman would use for a furrow plowed straight through a field. Paul is not telling Timothy to handle truth *carefully*. He is telling him to handle it *straight*—without bend, without flourish, without ornament that obscures the line.

This book attempts to *orthotomeō*. It is not interested in a clever angle on truth. It is interested in a straight one.

It is not written for the curious observer. It does not exist to persuade the skeptical or to entertain the distracted. It will not satisfy those looking for shortcuts, formulas, or rapid results.

It is written for those who have already paid a cost.

For those who have endured seasons that felt unnecessary to others.

For those who have learned to obey without affirmation.

For those who have allowed obscurity to shape them rather than embitter them.

This book is for those who recognize that restraint is not limitation, but wisdom.

It is for leaders who are tired of managing momentum and want to steward substance. For teachers who feel the weight of words and refuse to speak casually. For those who understand that access must be earned—not granted by enthusiasm alone.

It is also for those who have been hurt by unformed influence.

Those who have watched growth outpace wisdom. Those who have been affected by leadership that was effective but not anchored. Those who are cautious now—not because they are cynical, but because they are discerning.

This book is not accusatory.

It does not name names. It does not draw lines in public. It does not assign motives. Its purpose is not to expose people, but to clarify processes. It is meant to give language to instincts that were already present.

If you feel seen rather than stirred, this book is for you.

If you feel steadied rather than energized, this book is for you.

If you feel permission to slow down, to narrow focus, to guard what has been formed—this book is for you.

If, on the other hand, you feel irritated by the emphasis on restraint, or impatient with the pace, or resistant to the idea that not all growth should be trusted, this book may not be for you right now.

That is not a judgment.

It is timing.

This book will wait.

It is written to remain available when readiness catches up to desire. It will not chase attention. It will not reposition itself to be more appealing. It will simply remain, ready to be received by those who are prepared to carry what it describes.

This book is for those who are no longer asking how far they can go—but how faithfully they can stand.

And for those readers, nothing more needs to be said.

There is a moment in the Hebrew Scriptures that captures this kind of locating speech.

When Moses prepared to die, he gathered the tribes and spoke a blessing over each one. He did not give the same word to every tribe. Reuben got one word. Judah got another. Levi got another still. Each blessing was specific. Each word found *its* tribe and would have been wasted on any other.

Some words are like that.

They are not for everyone. They are for someone.

If this book has found you, it is because you were already standing where it was meant to land. The recognition you feel reading it is not because the writing is unusually persuasive. It is because the soil of your own life has already been prepared to receive what is being said.

The Hebrew word for that kind of recognition is *hineni* (הִנֵּנִי, Strong's H2009 with H589)—*here am I*. It is what Abraham said when God called. It is what Moses said at the burning bush. It is what Samuel said in the night when he was a boy in the temple. It is what Isaiah said when the seraphim filled the throne room and the question came: *Whom shall I send?*

Hineni is not a casual word. It is the answer of someone who recognizes the voice and is willing to be located by it.

If this book has caused you to say, even quietly, *Hineni*—here I am—then it has done its full work.

You are seen.

You are not alone in choosing roots over recognition.

And the One who has called you to this kind of formation is faithful, and He will do it (1 Thessalonians 5:24).

Chapter Twenty-One
Staying Rooted When Fruit Increases

Increase changes pressure.

When fruit multiplies, demands follow. Attention grows. Expectations rise. What was once simple becomes layered. What was once quiet begins to draw response. This is often the moment when roots are tested most.

Increase does not create instability.

It reveals it.

Staying rooted when fruit increases requires intentional restraint. It resists the urge to expand simply because expansion is possible. It refuses to let response dictate direction. It remembers that what produced the fruit must continue to be protected if the fruit is to remain healthy.

Roots are not strengthened by applause.

They are strengthened by consistency.

As fruit increases, the temptation is to adjust pace, posture, or message to accommodate demand. Invitations multiply. Requests increase. Opportunities appear reasonable—even beneficial. But not every opportunity is aligned, and not every request is a responsibility.

The Hebrew word for *increase* is *rabah* (רָבָה, Strong's H7235)—meaning *to multiply, to become great, to grow numerous.* It is the word God used over Abraham's descendants and over the fruitfulness commanded at creation. *Rabah* is a blessing.

But *rabah* is also dangerous when it outruns the soil.

Hosea warned an ancient Israel that had experienced *rabah* without root: *The more they multiplied, the more they sinned against Me; I will change their glory into shame* (Hosea 4:7). The increase itself was not the problem. What it revealed was.

Staying rooted requires returning again and again to first principles.

What did obedience look like before there was fruit?

What disciplines sustained formation before there was visibility?

What boundaries protected clarity when no one was watching?

Those practices must not be abandoned when fruit appears. They must be guarded more carefully than before.

Increase introduces noise.

Opinions multiply. Feedback intensifies. Expectations become external rather than internal. Without discernment, it becomes easy to confuse response with direction and demand with assignment.

Roots silence this confusion.

They anchor decision-making below the surface. They keep identity settled when attention fluctuates. They prevent reaction from replacing obedience.

Staying rooted also requires humility.

Fruit can tempt ownership. It can subtly shift perspective from stewardship to entitlement. When this happens, formation stalls. What once flowed freely becomes heavy. Joy is replaced by pressure.

Humility restores order.

It remembers that fruit is the result of abiding, not effort alone. It keeps gratitude intact. It resists comparison. It allows pruning without resentment.

Pruning often accompanies increase.

What is unnecessary is removed. What is distracting is cut back. This is not loss—it is preservation. Pruning makes room for strength to deepen so that future increase does not overwhelm the system that sustains it.

Those who remain rooted do not fear pruning.

They understand that reduction can strengthen longevity. They recognize that what is removed is often what would have drained energy or diluted focus later.

Staying rooted also means accepting limits.

Increase will always present more options than capacity. Saying no becomes more frequent. Access becomes more selective. Time becomes more valuable. These limits are not signs of withdrawal— they are signs of stewardship.

Roots thrive within boundaries.

They deepen where they are planted. They do not chase every source of nourishment. They grow steadily in the soil that has proven faithful.

If fruit is increasing in your life, resist the urge to expand prematurely. Protect the practices that formed you. Guard the boundaries that preserved clarity. Remain attentive to the quiet work beneath the surface.

Fruit that remains is sustained by roots that are continually tended.

Remain in truth.

Remain in obedience.

Remain in formation.

When fruit increases, return to the root.

That is where strength is renewed.

That is where clarity is preserved.

That is where what remains is secured.

There is a Hebrew word for the kind of person who can carry increase without being undone by it: *tzaddik* (צַדִּיק, Strong's H6662)—*the righteous one*. The Hebrew Scriptures say of him: *The righteous will flourish like the palm tree, he will grow like a cedar in Lebanon… they will still yield fruit in old age; they shall be full of sap and very green* (Psalm 92:12, 14).

The palm and the cedar are interesting choices.

The palm bends. The cedar stands.

The palm gives constantly—every part of the tree is useful, from fruit to fronds to fiber. The cedar holds firm—its wood was used for the very Temple in Jerusalem.

The *tzaddik*, the rooted one, holds both. He gives without being depleted. He stands without being rigid. He yields fruit *in old age*, when other trees have already stopped bearing.

This is the picture of fruit that remains.

Not the burst of an early harvest.

Not the spectacle of a single season.

But the long, steady, sap-filled fruitfulness of a tree God Himself planted, and that He intends to keep producing through every season of your life until the very last one.

Closing Reflection

This book was written to clarify, not to convince.

To protect, not to provoke.

To name what many have sensed but could not articulate.

If it has slowed you down, it has done its work.

If it has narrowed your focus, it has served its purpose.

If it has given you permission to value roots over recognition, it has landed where it was meant to.

There is one word that has run quietly under every chapter of this book—a word that has carried the whole weight of what we have been saying.

Shoresh (שֹׁרֶשׁ, Strong's H8328)—root.

It appears throughout the Hebrew Scriptures in places we sometimes pass too quickly. *He shall be like a tree planted by the waters, that spreads out its roots* (Jeremiah 17:8). *A shoot will spring forth from the stem of Jesse, and a branch from his roots will bear fruit* (Isaiah 11:1). *And those who escape from the house of Judah will again take root downward and bear fruit upward* (2 Kings 19:30).

Take root downward. Bear fruit upward.

The Hebrew mind never separated those two motions.

Roots first. Fruit second. Always in that order. Always.

What grows quickly will always attract attention.

What grows deeply will always endure.

Choose depth.

Choose formation.

Choose what remains.

Acknowledgments

To the Father, who plants what He intends to keep, and uproots what He never planted—thank You for the slow work. For the hidden years. For the seasons no one celebrated but You.

To Yeshua, the *Tsemach Tsaddiq*—the Righteous Branch—who came up out of dry ground and refused to grow in any soil but Your Father's. Every page of this book is an attempt to follow You where You have already walked.

To the Ruach HaKodesh, who has been the Teacher in every quiet place—thank You for the *qol demamah daqah*, the still small voice that has formed me when no one was watching.

To my family—thank you for loving me through every season the Lord has carried me through. You have been the soil where roots could grow.

To the Truths Coming and 818 Remnant community, and to every reader who has walked with the work of Truths Coming Inc.— thank you for choosing depth in a world that rewards spectacle. Your faithfulness is its own quiet harvest.

And to the reader holding this book—thank you for being willing to slow down. May what is rooted in you remain. May what is not, fall away in mercy.

About the Author

Cheri B is an author, songwriter, theologian, ordained minister and visual artist whose work spans the natural and the spiritual. She holds a Master of Divinity in Pastoral Theology and is the cofounder of Truths Coming Inc., a ministry rooted in Messianic and Hebrew Roots theology with a particular love for the appointed times and the ancient Hebraic mind.

She is the founder of Remnant Recordings, an independent worship label, and has released more than thirty original songs blending Hebrew language, prophetic worship, and the unhurried weight of the Spirit. She leads and teaches via online classes through Truths Coming and the 818 Remnant community, a faith-based traveling ministry for those drawn to depth, formation, and the slower work of God.

Cheri writes from the conviction that what God plants quietly, He sustains permanently—and that the most enduring fruit is grown in the seasons no one is watching.

She lives and ministers from a place of rest, building both with her hands and with her pen, in the natural and the spiritual.

Connect with her work at TruthsComing.com and CheriB.me.

Also by Cheri B

Other titles from Cheri B and Truths Coming Inc.:

From Death to Harvest

Resurrection, First Fruits, and the Road to Shavuot

A Messianic teaching tracing the fifty days from Resurrection to Pentecost—and the deep biblical pattern of harvest hidden inside them.

HaMashiach Mille et HaHaggadah shel Pesach

The Messiah Fills the Passover Haggadah

A Messianic Passover Haggadah grounded in Hebrew sources, drawing the Lamb out of every cup, every blessing, and every step of the Seder.

The Sound, the Blood & The Dwelling

Contemplative readings on presence, covenant, and abiding.

Times of Reflection

A devotional pairing times of day with Scripture, helping readers discern meaning in repeating number patterns. (Forthcoming, Redemption Press.)

Music from Remnant Recordings is available on Spotify, Apple Music, and major streaming platforms. Visit CheriB.me for the full catalog of books, music, and teachings.